CHRISTIAN WOMEN

Seraphim George

All rights reserved. No part of the material protected by this copyright notice may be reproduced or utilized in any form or by any means, electronic or mechanical, including photocopying, recording, or by any information storage and retrieval system, without written permission from the copyright owner.

This play is fully protected under copyright. No performance, professional or amateur, may be given without prior written consent of the author. To obtain permission(s) to use material from this work, please
email your request to seraphimgeorge@gmail.com

ISBN: 979-8-9998878-1-8

Copyright © 2025, Seraphim George

To my beloved mother, Cecilia,
a true saint-in-the-making,
and all-too-familiar with the arena.

INTRODUCTION

Christian Women was written out of a fascination with endurance; not just the endurance of faith, but the endurance of bodies, voices, and convictions in a world that does not welcome them. The early centuries of the Church are filled with names, half-stories, and fragments of women who endured persecution but very rarely were allowed to speak in their own right. *The Diary of St. Perpetua* is one rare exception to the rule, and when I read it the first time it gripped me. I could not understand the kind of faith that could turn a small, young girl into a historical giant.

Still, whether or not these early martyrs left their mark in history, in the liturgies and traditions of the historical Christian Church, their presence and defiance resound. I wanted to imagine them not as hagiography but as literature; alive with fear, desire, grief, and defiance, and though these characters are heavily based on historical people, I took many creative liberties, as one might when sequestering real, complex lives into the prison bars of a small book. My hope is that it will inspire Christians and non-Christians alike to look further into these women's lives, even if it is for a quick jaunt through a Wikipedia page.

The play does not ask for reverence so much as attention. The questions it wrestles with—how conviction survives in the face of cruelty, how love and loyalty hold under pressure, how the powerless resist the machinery of empire—are questions that belong to every reader, regardless of belief. In that sense, I see this play less as religious testimony and more as an act of literary recovery, giving dramatic shape to silences that resonate across time. Though the setting is ancient, the emotions are immediate, and they should prompt each of us to ask what we are living for and *why*, and if what we are living for is worth dying for.

Christian Women is based on the structure of Euripides' *Trojan Women*, which remains one of the great works of tragic endurance. Like Euripides, I was interested in the chorus of those defeated, particularly in the often overlooked stories of early Christian martyrdom and the way that, whether in Troy or Carthage, collective suffering becomes a kind of truth-telling.

Christian Women can be read as literature in its own right, standing alongside the tradition of works that bring the margins to the center. Whether one reads it as history reimagined or as a meditation on suffering, I pray the voices of these women reach beyond their time to touch ours. For those approaching it on the stage: the play is meant to be spoken plainly. The grandeur lies not in ornament but in the rawness of human voices caught between terror and faith. It is my hope that *Christian Women* will invite both readers and performers to feel that tension, and to honor the courage it demands.

DRAMATIS PERSONAE

VIBIA PERPETUA	young Christian noble woman; mother of Marcus; daughter of Petrus Romanus
FELICITAS	handmaid to Perpetua; nurse to Marcus
REVOCATUS	servant of Perpetua's household
PUDENS	pagan soldier; assistant overseer of the prison
ABDESHMUN	high priest of Eshmun; pagan oracle
PUBLIUS HILARIANUS	procurator of Carthage
SATURUS	a deacon of the church at Carthage
MARCUS	son of Perpetua
APOLLONIA	ex-wife of Hilarianus; mother of Cecilia
CECILIA	daughter of Hilarianus and Apollonia.
TERTIUS VULSO	commanding officer in the Carthaginian army
PETRUS ROMANUS	Roman senator; father of Perpetua.
FAUSTINA SULLA	wife of Hilarianus
MISC. ATTENDANTS	(nonspeaking)

ACT 1

Scene: The year is 200 AD. Carthage, still reeling from the Antonine Plague twenty years earlier, has just been hit with an earthquake. Citizens are looking for someone to blame, and under the Roman Emperor Septimus Severus, a great persecution of Christians has commenced.

On this day, the birthday of the emperor's younger brother Geta Caesar is to be celebrated with different festivities throughout the city. In a prison beneath a Carthaginian arena, huddled in groups around the stage, are Christian women, asleep. Among them are PERPETUA and her friend APOLLONIA, two noblewomen imprisoned with their children MARCUS and CECILIA. They are dressed in the tatters of once elegant gowns.

PERPETUA, a woman in her early twenties, is awakened by a dream and begins to reflect on her own and her people's fate. She addresses her thoughts to the audience, conscious somehow that God and posterity will be watching her.

Perpetua: Everything my hands have made, all I had, was lost to circumstance. Whoever trusts in sovereignty, whoever fears neither God nor gods but finds solace in his strength, look at me. I bear in me a message: in a moment it can all be gone. And like me, Carthage also fell: first to plagues and now to earthquakes, and it is the Christians at whose doorstep blame is laid. Our home is now our prison; our friends enemies; our pride is now our shame.

I call to witness the so-called divinity of the gods, who are hostile to me and the ashes of my country. I call to witness those who dwell deep beneath the Roman realm, waiting to receive our blood. The gods do not dwell on Mt. Olympus but in the depths of Hades. They are murderers, destroyers of free conscience. Watch and learn: I will never bow to you, cruel divinities, uncaring fates. You speak through those I love, you tempt me to undo my vows of faith and battle against my own heart. What are you so afraid of? That there is freedom in Rome? That there are those who ruin your empire? By doing what? Caring for the sick, giving alms to the poor and teaching all that God is love? Your priests do none of these things, all supposed crimes worthy of death. No, I have committed no crime.

But these things I remember as I pour out my soul: how I used to go to the house of God under His protection, with shouts of joy and praise among the festive throng.

Why, my soul, are you so afraid? Why so disturbed within me? Put your hope in God, for I will yet praise Him, my Savior and my god.

Felicitas: By day the Lord directs His love. At night His song is with me - a prayer to the god of my life. I say to God my Rock, "Why have you forgotten me? Why must I go about mourning, oppressed by the enemy?" My bones suffer mortal agony as my foes taunt me, saying to me all day long, "Where is your God?"

Perpetua: Felicitas, you're awake.

Felicitas: Yes. I heard you as you prayed. Could you not sleep?

Perpetua: Felicitas, tonight I had a dream. I should recount it, so that I never forget that God spoke to me. You see, yesterday, when my brother came to visit me, he said, "Dear sister, you are already in a position of great dignity and have received access to the god's will. Ask him for a vision, that it may be made known to you whether this imprisonment will result in death, in slavery, or in escape." And I was given the faith to ask with confidence, for his kindnesses to me have always been great. And this was what was shown me on this very night.

I saw a golden ladder reaching up even into the Realm that is higher than Olympus, and it was very narrow, so that a person could only ascend it one by one; and on the ladder's sides was every kind of weapon, so that if any one went up carelessly, he would be torn to pieces. And under the ladder was crouching a dragon of monstrous size, who lay in wait for those who were called to ascend, frightening all who saw it. And my teacher, Saturus, who is imprisoned with us now, went up first and reached the top, from where he turned and cried, "Perpetua, I wait for you, but be careful that the dragon does not bite you." I replied, "In the name of the Lord Jesus Christ, he will not hurt me." As soon as the words were spoken, the great dragon lowered its head, and I stepped upon it, and ascended the ladder. When I reached the top I saw another world, as if beneath the veil of this world, and in the new world I saw a garden, and in the midst of it, a shepherd surrounded by many sheep, who were happily eating and at rest. And his eyes caught mine, and his face was the face of God, for it was the image of God; that is, Christ, the Lord. "Come," he said to me, holding out his hand, "you are welcome here, my daughter. Come and rest with me upon this pasture, and I will care for you." And then I awoke.

Felicitas: Then you will die, like the rest of us.

Perpetua: I do not know. I do not know where the message came from. For I heard tell that the noble women will not die but will be made slaves. But I would rather leave this realm, for what god receives mere mortals and does not relegate them to Hades?

And I think my spirit tells me that tomorrow I *will* die. It will grow darker still, for us, before it grows light again. As cruel as they have been, we have not yet seen the dragon.

Felicitas: Why do you speak to me as if I am overwhelmed by fear? I am no untrained stranger to tears that you bid me be prepared. This we have all done for months unceasing. But I am prepared, for the god came to me last night as well. In a dream, I was thrown to the arena, commanded to fight a tall and muscular Egyptian, a gladiator, whom I knew to be the Devil. I was mortally wounded by his sword, and yet, before I died, I cut off his head. So I know whenever it comes, death will find me, and still I am ready. We suffer at the hands of our own people, persecuted and tortured because we love and follow another god, but it is the Devil who persecutes us. Now it will be my turn to face him. Common slave as I am, I will follow my mistress; if your dream is true, you will not die alone.

Perpetua: Oh, trusted sister, pray that you *will* die, for if condemned to be the slave of another, they will not treat you as I have. In the day this happens, unbind your locks; over shoulders weak with sobs let them flow, defiled by the warm dust of Carthage. They will give you away to men who will use your body as a toy, who will make you fornicate and be to them a whore, though in your heart you are pure, untouched. You and all the Christian women here will laugh recalling the days you touted your chastity and boasted at your purity, for you will let down your robes for them; and if you resist, then steel yourself for the rain of mad blows that will be loosed upon you. No, repeat once more your old lamentations if you are not condemned to die.

Felicitas: Do not say those things. They will not happen to you. If not death, then God will allow you a good master, one who is as kind to you as you have been to me.

O grief, put forth your strength. Let all Africa echo with your wails. Let them all hear how they have treated the innocent. Let every sea hear us, and every sky, and all the dying gods, let them hear our cries. Let them witness this final act of humiliation.

O, Perpetua . . .

Perpetua: It is for you that my hands grip my stomach and my bleeding shoulders shake, because you have never been just a servant to me, but a sister. That is what you are to me, and how I would spare my sister this.

And look, in the corner: my son. O Marcus, I weep for you as well, my love, my bright shining star. I can only pray they will let you live and not send you on the road your father traveled. But their vengeance at his treachery is great, and they might destroy you too. It is for you my hand beats my head; for you my breasts with a mother's palms are mangled.

O gods of Rome, will you never let us be? You are the head of an empire, yet you are a hindrance to the greatest emperor, you who should have been a refuge to the weary. You have wasted my country's walls when Hannibal came against you. A thousand years she stood; with you she fell, and now again you come against her people.

Revocatus: My lady, what is wrong? Why is this night different than any other night?

Perpetua: O Revocatus, everything is wrong. I feel that something darker than we have yet seen is coming and sooner than we feared. I wish I never woke you, so you could continue in your sleep. But soon enough you will rest again.

Revocatus: I am ready. Believe me that I am. And all of Carthage, all of Rome, all the earth will receive the sound of this injustice, and slave though I am, they will remember. Oh Christ, will the torment never cease? You suffered only for a little while, and we still suffer. A hundred years or more, and we still suffer. Who can stand it? Yet, I am ready.

Perpetua: You are very brave. Yet, do not trouble your heart with doubt. Our suffering will be made light. Remember how he cried and how he sweat drops of blood; remember he was beaten and mocked as we have been; remember he was crucified, all for the joy set before him.

Let us mourn no longer; rather, let us rejoice and turn our tears, no longer pitying our fates. Cry out "Oh, happy day!", for we are being sent not to the land of gloom and ghosts, hidden deep beneath the earth but to a god who receives us on high and knows our names. Remember how he chose his fate for our sakes, and we will do the same for him. We are like cattle that don their yokes willingly; we do not struggle, for when our work is done we go to lie in green pastures.

Revocatus:	Then "Happy day!" I say. We both will, won't we, Felicitas? Happy day!
	In departing, he has taken his kingdom. Now he waits in the other realm for the day he shall return. It is in Eden that he waits, and we will go there and wait with him. So happy day indeed. And happy are we. For with his death, he has made an end of all.
	(Enter PUDENS, pagan soldier and prison overseer.)
Pudens:	Perpetua, come; I must speak with you alone. I carry dark news. If you have found some respite in this night, I pray your god has made it full.
Revocatus:	Look you, pagan! A slave I might be, but my mistress is my sister in this dungeon and in death. I will not be left out. Come out with it! Tell us this dark news.
Pudens:	Very well, slave. But I must tell you it is for Perpetua that my spirit is most afraid, for she has welcomed me, though I am not like her.

Perpetua, something is happening beyond which I could have expected. I expected more time. But I have seen it, the wrath of the gods. It came to me in a dream. The sea, vast before me, lay like glass belying the turmoil underneath. This sea was black, like coal, and I stood upon its shore. Then a god rose from it, monstrous in size. I saw that it was Cronos, that mighty titan who destroyed his father. He was like an old man, and in one hand he held a child, one of the other gods, and was devouring the baby, for fear that it would grow up and do to him what he had done to his Creator. And when he was finished, he threw the remains of the god into the water and a great earthquake began and the sea rose up where the child had fallen and rushed towards shore. Then from his mouth a black cloud erupted, spewing forth a plague. And in his other hand I saw a cross, and filled with rage he broke it, all the while piercing me with his murderous sight. I awoke, greatly afraid.

I did not understand the dream, other than it was an ill omen for the Christians, but then yesterday, I was to serve as gatekeeper to Hilarianus, and I overheard him speaking to someone clothed in a dark cloak. A god had appeared in the temple of Tanit, the goddess. I do not know which one. The god revealed to the oracles that the earthquake and the plagues came to Carthage because of the Christians, who have refused to pay homage. They demand a sacrifice on the Caesar's birthday: today. Today, you will be taken before Hilarianus and he will pass judgment on you if you confess the new religion.

I thought we had more time to plead your case, Perpetua, for the nobles are often granted reprieve of their crimes, especially for the sake of your father, so highly regarded.

Perpetua: But I have committed no crime. Is it a crime to think independently of the State, or to worship a god of one's own choosing? What have we done to deserve this, Pudens? The Christians pay their taxes. They are known in all the land for doing only good. And they repay us for our good works by burning us with fire and boiling oil, by flaying us alive, by throwing us to wild beasts, by crucifying us.

Pudens: But the one god you choose to worship is the Caesar of all the heavens. He is not like the others, and our Caesar and his gods will not bear it.

(Exit PUDENS, PERPETUA, REVOCATUS, FELICITAS *and the other prisoners.)*

ACT II

Scene: The city hall, the judicial court and seat of the Carthaginian procurator. HILARIANUS *is reclining on the judgment seat or walking about listening as* ABDESHMUN, *high priest of Eshmun, rails at him.*

Abdeshmun: Still you cannot see what you must do? Why this weakness, Hilarianus? It is not becoming of a Carthaginian. We were sons of Baal, gods of the earth in that land far across the sea. Our people were once enemies of the Jews who dwelt there, and the Jewish god, who plagues us still by these Christians, was the enemy of our gods. But our deities prevailed, making Tyre into a great city-state, while the Jews were trampled and dispersed, their temples destroyed.

Then when the god Melquart was insulted by the king, he sent those faithful to the old ways across the sea to populate the land. We landed here, in Africa, under our Queen Elissar. Her blood flows in your veins,

Hilarianus. Her wisdom. Years after, she won the great hill from our enemies, establishing our kingdom. We kept building on her legacy, conquering our neighbors and became the shining city that ruled all Africa. Remember how strong we once were.

Yes, Carthage fell to the Romans. Hannibal was destroyed. Yet from the ashes we rose again, did we not? We were a phoenix among flames. We must not forget. The gods would not have our destruction. The Romans built us up again, greater than we were even in our golden age. So we have been to this day.

But now, what with the plagues that destroyed a third of our people and now the earthquake, we are being destroyed again. The gods are being replaced, our priests disenfranchised, and the temple services are ending because people worship the dying god.

Who ever heard of a dying god? Yet they fawn over this Jewish bastard as if he were Zeus! I will never understand it. He lacks something. The panache of the old gods, the victorious wrath and fearful devotion divinity deserves. It is as if they defaced the Jewish god, so the being he became is utterly unlike the god of old, this effeminate Christ. At least the Jews still worship the right sort, and they still receive their blessings from him and from the Empire. But this new god, or whatever he is, this is a god who will make our men women and our women men.

You know that Melquart, the ancient one, came to us in the temple of Tanit. I have not even had a visit from Eshmun, and yet this king of gods visits me. He is angry with this new religion and demands their sacrifice. You must declare your verdict over them and be done with it, before you single-handedly destroy Carthage once again for the sake of these heretics.

This great overthrow of nations, this widespread terror of the gods, all the land wrecked as by a single blast, to any other god could have been considered the pinnacle of might; but to Hammon, Tanit, and Melquart they are but deeds along the way. I am proud to recount my great divinity's glorious deeds: your wife, Faustina, healed by Eshmun after my sacrifices and prayers. You are his debtor, if rightly you estimate his worth, even if he should ask for one of your own daughters. Remember the sign given to you in the temple to confirm that it was the deity who spoke. Remember what he asks of you.

Hilarianus: (*inwardly*) Why do you torment me, Deshmun? I am tired of arguing with you. After Minucias died, I found myself upon the judgment's seat and deemed unfit to rule. You take advantage of this for your own games, you serpent. I know what is in your mind, and it is not justice for Carthage. The love of the gods cannot touch you. You know that it was the god of the Christians who healed Faustina when you and your priests could not. You do not serve Eshmun, but Invidia. Jealousy moves your heart to violence, and ungoverned violence is folly; in the case of others, it is the first fervor of their years that sweep them on, but with you it is your own pride.

And yet, he does not lie. The great god of Carthage did give me a sign. He asks me for the one I used to call daughter. Why does he besmirch the noble line of Carthage with this cruel bloodshed?

(*to* ABDESHMUN) Thank you, priest, for your lesson in history. But you should remain in your temple and leave the teaching to the teachers. If you were fit to teach on Carthage, you would see that it was Scipio who brought our city down to Hades with violence, and not with mercy, with rape, and pillaging, and the murder of our children, the burning of our temples and our homes. That was his legacy. Those were the ashes out of which we had to rise.

So I have a lesson for you. It is fitting for you to first learn what the victor ought to do to the vanquished. Ungoverned power can not be retained for long; controlled, it lasts; and the higher Fortune has raised and exalted the might of man, the more does it become him to be modest in prosperity, to tremble at shifting circumstances, and to fear the gods when they are over kind. I was a general once. I know how greatness can be in a moment overthrown. You forget that we are no longer Carthaginians. We are Romans standing on the bones of Carthage.

It is true: in the past we have dealt harshly with dissenters, but I am not alone among our leaders and philosophers who despise the torture of prisoners and the bloodlust of the games, even though the crowds demand it. The worst in man makes it so. Should we cater to the worst in man, even if the gods demand it? Are not the gods simply men elevated to immortality, but men just the same?

For my part, I will confess that I wished to see the Christians beaten down and conquered for the sake of the Empire, if for nothing else. And I *have* imprisoned them and beaten them for their incessant proselytizing; but tortured and utterly destroyed--would that I would spare them that. All that can survive of them, let them survive; enough punishment has been enacted. That a pious maiden should fall, I will not permit. The blame of it all comes back on me; he who, when he may, does not stop evil, is guilty of it.

Abdeshmun: And shall the god have no satisfaction?

Hilarianus: It shall; all shall sing of Baal Hammon. The Romans know him as Cronos, but they will soon know he comes from Carthage, not Rome. They will hear his mighty name. But if his appetite can only be appeased by out-poured blood, then let our cattle be slain before the games, and let blood flow which will cause no mother's tears. Save her father from scorn and hate, brought on by the bidding of a maiden's death.

Abdeshmun: Is your heart suddenly inflamed with love for the wife you divorced and the daughter you disowned because of their faith? Or have you found your calling in this new religion and in hatred of the old ways? Will you single-handedly destroy us all by your blasphemous sentimentality?

Hilarianus: I do blaspheme. But the Christians say I do, and we say they do. All religion is the same. The gods all war with one another and will war until there are none left. Maybe then we shall have some peace. I think sometimes perhaps there are no gods.

Abdeshmun: But if you are wrong? I have spoken the truth. The gods of Rome reign. Remember the destruction of Jerusalem. Even the god of the Jews abandoned them and went over to the Romans. He abandons the Christians now, or he would have saved them.

Hilarianus: Yes. In that war, Rome found its peace in Palestine.

Abdeshmun: The gods declared it so. It is a high, kingly act to give peace to mere humans.

Hilarianus: Why then do they also take life, demand sacrifice, crave appeasement and yet offer no love, no solace? And why should I do the same?

Abdeshmun: Your old age has made you womanly. Remember, too, that the merciful will often give death instead of life. Think thusly if you must. Send them to their god, if they so long for it.

Hilarianus: And is it now for mercy's sake you seek my daughter for the tomb?

Abdeshmun: She is not your daughter anymore, simply a maid. You forfeited the right to call her daughter when you declared her and her mother enemies of Rome.

Hilarianus: To put country before family befits a king.

Abdeshmen: No law spares the captive or stays the penalty.

Hilarianus: But what the law does not forbid, shame and common decency forbids.

Abdeshmun: It is a god's right to do whatever he wills.

Hilarianus: Least should he will who has much right.

Abdeshmun: Do you dare fling such blasphemous words at those who have given you everything, have exalted you from servant, to soldier, to general, to procurator? What next, emperor? And would you still then repay the gods with your meekness?

Hilarianus: It is Severus who gave me this position. He is Caesar, not the gods, and he has refused to pass an edict against the Christians.

Abdeshmun: But he has left it up to each province to deal with them. And they refuse to burn incense to Caesar, so whether for the gods or for Caesar, the outcome is the same. Will you relinquish your rulership for the Christian god and his insane fanatics? Look how he treats his own followers, with contempt, abandonment, shame; neither does he save them from the fires or the wild beasts.

Hold a trial, declare the will of the gods, or you shall have a revolt on your hands in addition to whatever else Minucius left behind for you to do.

Hilarianus: (*inwardly*) You have received too much power far too young. So much passion, but scarce yet a man. You have yet to taste your mortality. When the gods are through with you, you will die like the rest of us. Hades will open its mouth to you, your intimacy with the gods to no avail. I could check your words and curb your disrespect, but my sword knows how to spare even fools. And alas! While alive he has the will of the people in his hands.

(*to* ABDESHMUN) So what, then, is the will of the gods?

Abdeshmun: Cecilia must be sacrificed this very afternoon, condemned to the beasts with the others. As your offspring, withholding mercy will mean much to the gods, since they have made you the African proconsul. And since it is on the birthday of the emperor's brother, her death will, all at once, be a show of loyalty to Rome, a sign of personal sacrifice, and a declaration against the Christians.

But she is not the only one who delays our prosperity; blood nobler than hers is also due. Among the prisoners is one Vibia Perpetua, the daughter of Petrus Romanus, who has already come to the city for his daughter. Her husband was crucified under Minucius. The offspring that bears his name must be sacrificed upon the burning hands of Cronos and dropped into the flames, as in the days of old. Then will the city be free of all its tribulation.

Hilarianus: The gods demand a high price. Go. Send for the woman and her son. Have them bring the slaves imprisoned with them. Send also for the teacher, the man called Saturus, and for her father, who is staying at the governor's house and should be here to witness his daughter's trial. Perhaps he will convince her to recant and stop this nonsense.

And do not bring Apollonia or the girl. Apollonia has already confessed and is condemned to servitude. That Cecilia has to die . . . I would rather leave it for Faustina to deliver the news to the mother.

If I condemn the others today, then I will send Tercius Vulso for the boy, that he may be brought to the sacrifice as the gods command.

Abdeshmun: What do you mean "if I condemn"?

Hilarianus: By the gods, you test my patience! I will not condemn them without a trial. There is a condition on this divine command or there is no obedience to it. I will ask them only to burn incense to the image of Caesar. They need not recant their faith, only throw the incense into the fire. If they do this, I will free them.

And do not look at me like that, Deshmun! You will do as I say, or I swear that I will have you killed, and the revolt I would face from your followers would be worth the spilling of your blood. I still have the power of life and death over you; the gods have given me at least that much.

Now get out of my sight!

(*Exit* ABDESHMUN)

(*inwardly*) Is it true that spirits live on when bodies have been buried or burned, when the wife has closed her husband's eyes, when the last day has blotted out the sun, when the mournful urn holds fast our ashes? Does it matter when we give up our souls to death in the hopes of living still longer? Or do we wholly die and does no part of us remain when with, our final breath, the spirit mingles with the air and the lighted fire has touched the naked body? Will we, as the the Jews and Christians profess, rather than enter into Hades, reclaim our bodies at their god's return? Do our bodies wait for our spirits at some as yet unforeseen day of judgment? Should we hope in some eternal kingdom? I'll give them this much: their god is more generous in death than ours.

Time, with the pace of Pegasus, shall gather us all in by the end of the matter. With such whirlwind speed as the twelve signs that fly along the night sky, with such swift course as the lord of stars hurries on his path, and in the same way the goddess Hecate hastens on her slanting road, so are we propelled towards fate, to peruse the faces of those three sisters, the last thing we shall see before we are extinguished. As smoke from burning fire vanishes, staining the air for one brief moment; as clouds are scattered by the cold blasts of Boreas, so shall the spirit that rules my body float away.

No. There is nothing after death, and death itself is nothing. Let the pious give up their hope; let the wicked give up their fear. Time and chaos engulf them both. Death does not need instruction; it is not picky; it kills the body and the soul. Cerberus, who guards the portal of the passage, is but an idle myth, an empty word, a tale fleeting as a morning dream.

You ask where you will be when you are dead? I will tell you. Where they are, who were never born.

(Enter PERPETUA, SATURUS, FELICITAS, REVOCATUS, and PETRUS ROMANUS accompanied by a small group of soldiers)

Hilarianus: *(To prisoners)* I will make this swift, but you have the power to make it painless. This is only to establish your guilt before the proconsul, and whether or not you are worthy of death.

You there, what is your name?

Saturus: I am called Saturus, lord.

Hilarianus: Come forward, Saturus. Are you their teacher? Are you the bishop of the Christian church in Carthage?

Saturus:	No, lord. I am a deacon serving under Agrippinus, who is bishop. But yes, I am teacher to these.
Hilarianus:	And is it true that you voluntarily gave yourself up to be here?
Saturus:	Yes.
Hilarianus:	But why? Do you not know there is a penalty of torture or even death?
Saturus:	You alone know that a good general enters into the fray along with his troops to, if not rescue them from peril, at least comfort them in the face of death and give them courage. I have been with them since before their baptisms, when all was well and we had peace. How could I not be with them now, in their suffering?
Hilarianus:	So, it was you who destroyed the nobility of lady Perpetua's household. Are you aware that you will be responsible for their deaths, that in fact, you are already responsible for her husband's crucifixion?
Saturus:	Are you responsible for the deaths of your soldiers when they follow you into the fray? I am no more responsible for their

deaths than you are for those who serve beneath you, and some of those are coerced into fighting by the State. My warriors choose freely to enter into battle.

Hilarianus: You are well spoken and seem to have a measure of wisdom. Let us see if you have wisdom for this: spare your own life, and I will have mercy on those who listen to your teaching.

(*to his attendants*) Bring the image, and set it before this man.

Now, burn incense to the image of Caesar as a god, and you will be freed. Moreover, you may continue to believe in your convictions. Simply pay homage to the State, and I will allow you the workings of your inner conscience. I am being more generous than others have been.

Saturus: Is it not reasonable to believe that your body and your heart are one? For if you desire in your mind to do something, then do you not do it? It is written that as a man thinks, so he becomes. How, then, can you ask me to pay homage with my hands but not my heart?

Therefore, I will not burn incense, for Caesar is not a god and never shall be. There is only one man who is worthy of worship, and he is God from the beginning and sits upon the throne of Heaven.

We do homage to Caesar by paying our taxes and being good citizens. Let that be enough.

Hilarianus: Then you are not as wise as I first thought. Saturus, according to your own words, then, do I condemn you. Tonight you shall be thrown to the wild beasts.

Saturus: So be it, lord. But do not forget that we have not thrown ourselves to the beasts by our confession, but it is you who throw us to the beasts. You judge us now, but it is God who will judge you, so remember our faces, that you may recognize them on the Day of Judgment.

Hilarianus: Be silent! Enough of your delusions.

It is my understanding that there are two slaves here from Perpetua's household. Step forward.

Now, listen to me carefully. You are only slaves. Your very lives bear witness to the disfavor of the gods. You have already heard that slaves are condemned to die when found guilty of various crimes. Yet I am merciful, so I will give even you a chance to spare your own lives. Burn incense to Caesar as god, even if, in your own minds, you still worship your Christ, and you will be spared.

Young lady, what is your name?

Felicitas: I am called Felicitas.

Hilarianus: And you are a slave, correct?

Felicitas: It is as you say, lord.

Hilarianus: And what is your confession?

Felicitas: That Jesus Christ is Lord, the Son of the living God.

Hilarianus: Then you will not burn incense?

Felicitas: I will not.

Hilarianus: Do you realize I have the power to free you? I need only say the word, and you will no longer be a slave.

Felicitas: Pardon me, but you are mistaken, lord. It is true we are called slaves, but the truth is that we are slaves no longer. Our king has made us free. In him there is neither slave nor freeman.

Hilarianus: Really? Have you received a declaration from Caesar? I had not heard.

Felicitas: Caesar is our governor, yes, but not our king. We have only one King: that is, Christ. And he has declared us free.

Hilarianus: You are all mad. Your Christ is dead. But so be it. See how much your freedom brings you in the arena.

And you, slave, do you say the same? Are you a Christian?

Revocatus: I am a Christian.

Hilarianus: Then you will suffer the same.

Now, lady Perpetua. You may come forward. Greet your father, or has he visited you before?

Perpetua: He has.

Hilarianus: And what did he say to you?

Perpetua: That I should repent of my ways. That I should have pity on his grey hairs and remember all the goodness he has done me, how he treated me as an equal to my brothers. That I should have regard for them and for my mother and especially for my son.

Hilarianus: And have you considered his words?

Perpetua: As always I consider what my father says, for he has a type of worldly wisdom that has served me well. But my conclusion remains the same, for I said to him that if we should be taken to you, then whatever God wills shall happen, for we are not placed in our own power, but in the power of God. And here I am.

(*spoken to* PETRUS ROMANUS) Papa, why do you come here a second time? Is it because you wish to see me condemned?

P. Romanus: Do not be a fool, Vibia! Of course, I do not want to see you condemned! I am here to beg you again, to implore you: relent! Stop this madness! You are killing our family, destroying the future of your son. Think of him! If he does not die, then he will have no reputation, will be no more than a slave, as you will be, because of the pride of your convictions.

I command you, burn incense to Caesar! Who cares about what the hand does? Cut off your hand if you so despise it for betraying your god. But now let your hand place the incense in the bowl, and move on with your life. For the smoke cannot touch your heart, where Christ still lives. Surely your god judges only the heart.

Perpetua: My heart grieves for you. In it there is only sorrow, and I would spare you such suffering. But you do not understand how it is we live. For our god is not like the gods of Rome, who care only for the external trappings of religion. Our god is judge of both the body and the soul. If I burn incense with my hand, yet my heart remains faithful to God, still I sin, for it is God who made the hand. And if I do not

	burn incense, yet in my heart desire to burn it to spare my own life, then still I sin, for it is God who made the heart. Therefore, I do not burn incense to Caesar, both with my hand and with my heart.
P. Romanus:	(*throwing himself before* PERPETUA) But do you not understand? You are killing me, your own father! You will drive me to my grave. Let go of your contempt for life, and think of me. Think of your son!
Perpetua:	Please! Papa, you must stop this! You must find your peace. It is better for me to die nobly than to die ignobly. And it is not me who has a contempt for life, but those who condemn us to death when we have done no wrong. Look here. Papa, what is that upon the pillar?
P. Romanus:	A vase.
Perpetua:	And would it be madness to say that it is a vase when others say it is a donkey? Can a vase be anything other than a vase?
P. Romanus:	No.

Perpetua: Then neither can I be anything other than a Christian.

Hilarianus: Your husband has already received the benefit of his confession, crucified at the city gates. For the love of your god, Perpetua, even I implore you to listen to your father. Spare his gray hairs; spare the life of your boy; offer sacrifice to the Emperor. If you do not, your son will die, and you will become a childless slave.

Perpetua: I will not burn incense. If my son dies, then it will not be for my sins but for yours. What have we done that is so horrible it merits torture and death? But the Christians have done nothing but good. Tell me, what crime have I committed? What crime has my son, only ten years old, committed against the emperor? What crime have we all committed other than to live simply, love our neighbors, and do good to strangers and orphans and widows? It is more than your priests ever do, much more than your gods ever demand.

Hilarianus: You ask what crime? Why, the crime of confessing to be a Christian!

Perpetua: But I am a Christian.

(at this PETRUS ROMANUS *throws himself at her and begins to yell at her and beat her, after which the soldiers pull him off and begin to beat him with a rod*)

Hilarianus: Enough of this! Get them out of my sight! They will all receive from their god exactly what they deserve.

ACT III

Scene: In the dungeon PUDENS, APOLLONIA, CECILIA, *and* MARCUS *are still there, waiting for the others to return from their trial when* PERPETUA, SATURUS, FELICITAS, *and* REVOCATUS *enter.* PERPETUA *runs to her son and holds him close.*

Marcus: What is wrong, mother? Why are you weeping?

Apollonia: Yes, my God, she can hardly speak. Saturus, what did that devil, my husband, do to you?

Saturus: Perpetua. Perpetua, do not weep so.

Why do you shed tears unrestrained? If our sufferings can be measured only by tears, then they are surely trivial. Yes, this is a hard blow, and we have fallen. But for you; for me, we fell long since, when they condemned your husband and my friend to crucifixion. On that day, overwhelmed and ruined, whatever has happened since I

	bear, numb with woe and insensible. But now, escaping the Romans, I will follow your husband and there, before the Lord, will tell him of all that has happened. And so, too, will his son, and how happy will they be when they meet.
Pudens:	His son? What do you mean his son? Have they condemned Marcus too?
Saturus:	A greater woe from woe arises. The hunger of the gods is not yet stayed. More evil than a martyr's death, he will be sacrificed to an idol, as in the days of old in Carthage, when children were given to the gods as food. Death surely is impartial, and yet to be eaten by the gods! That terror disturbs alone, but that it should happen to one of us is too much to bear.
Perpetua:	(*still holding* MARCUS) O son, true offspring of a mighty sire, sole comfort of our stricken house, too like your father; such features did he have, such was his gait; his brave hands, his shoulders set high and proud, so august, you have them all. My son, born too late for nobility, too soon for your mother, it is unjust that you should die like this, for I did not conceive that they would go so far as to condemn you after

having condemned your father. My only consolation is that you will be spared the sufferings brought on by life, the torment endured by those who choose to bear the name Christ. Now you will be with the one for whom we all suffer.

And yet, I wonder if there is perhaps a chance that you might live. Perhaps your life would not be so full of evil, for even Felicitas has had a child, a little girl who is now cared for by a Christian sister as if she were the child's mother. But where would I hide you? What place shall I choose to cheat them? For Rahab the prostitute deceived the soldiers searching for the Jews, all the while hiding those two poor men, so that their enemies would go elsewhere. And though she lied, the god who hates a lying tongue still blessed her, for she had lied to save his people. In the same way could I save you now.

Felicitas: Yes, it just might work. Seize any refuge.

Pudens: And for you, my lady, I would surely take him out from here, find a place that is safe where he can live. But now, go quickly, hide him! I have heard the voice of Tercius

	Vulso. He is here to take the boy! Hide him, and then after I will help him to escape.
Perpetua:	But if the foe inquires?
Apollonia:	Lie, for God's sake! Lie! He perished in the earthquake, lost with all the other children of Carthage who perished; this cause alone has saved many from destruction--the belief that they are dead. And Tercius Vulso does not know your son.
Perpetua:	Scant hope is left; the crushing weight of his nobility lies heavy on him. What will it profit him to be hidden, when he must fall into their hands?
	(*to* MARCUS) What place, what spot, remote and least expected, will keep you safe? O Christ, who always shields your own, shield him now! I shudder to think of where I must place you, but in the pits there, the latrines where falls the prisoners' excrement. They will not expect you there, but in every other room and box and barrel they would look. O son, that you would be covered by such filth, that precious face defiled. But perhaps it is a way.

Pudens will help lower you, my son. Just be still, and after I will make sure that you are clean for your escape.

(PERPETUA *and* PUDENS *begin to lead* MARCUS *offstage*)

Why do you shrink back? Is it the vile stench of the place?

Ah, yes. I recognize your noble birth. You are ashamed of fear. You wish to be like your father. But again, this may not be your time to die. Put away your high spirit and courage; put on such spirit as misfortune grants. Come, like our Lord, the one whom you have always loved, enter into this, the filth of human waste. Who knows what good will come if you survive?

(MARCUS is led offstage by PUDENS)

Felicitas: (*To* PERPETUA) Let the foul pit protect its charge; and so that your fear does not give him away, retreat into a corner. Withdraw so that they may not see your face.

Apollonia: (*To* PERPETUA) I will address the general in your stead, my sister. Do not fear. You have suffered greatly, and since it is not my own child facing death but yours, perhaps it will be easier for me to hide my terror. (*She looks behind her and sees* TERCIUS VULSO *approaching*)

Felicitas: (*To* PERPETUA) Be still a little while, my love. Utter not a word or cry; the army's leader comes. You shall be Apollonia. She shall be Perpetua. He knows not which one is the condemned's mother.

Stand back Saturus. Stand with your disciple. It is better that he sees a woman's face.

Perpetua: (*with a final appealing look to where her son is hiding*) Be still, my little one. Be still, as if asleep and the earth covers you. Lord, hide the charge I give you, for our enemy is here; in his heart he weaves some crafty tactic for our doom.

(*Enter* TERCIUS VULSO)

T. Vulso: As a minister of fate, I beg this first: although these words are uttered by my lips, you count them not my words; it is not my voice but the voice of all Rome that brings my news. I am told you have a son, and I must take him; the fates demand him.

Apollonia: Are you, then, a Christian too, that you pretend to have such charity? Why do you care about our pain?

T. Vulso: I am no Christian. But I was a gladiator, and I know what it is to be a slave condemned to death, and to be an enemy of Rome. But you will be robbed even of the dignity of fighting for your life, though I am told your people face death unafraid.

The mistrust of uncertain peace will always possess Rome, and fear will force her to look behind and not let them lay down their arms against the Christians, so long as nobles convert and the subversive religion conquers.

Are you the mother?

Apollonia: I am.

T. Vulso: You think I have no heart, because I am a pagan. You believe that only your god knows what kindness is, and mercy. This is not true. But I know that duty trumps these both.

I am a slave again, in deed. I do what I must. Grief is no impartial judge; still, if you weighed the matter within yourself, you would forgive a soldier who does what he is told. And think me not cruel because, at the bidding of the lot, I seek your son.

Now, perhaps if you recant your faith, your baby might be spared. There is still time, and Hilarianus will take my word that you are willing to burn incense to Caesar. But I will not lie. You must do it.

Apollonia: O that I could burn incense to save my son, for I am sick of our god. I have served him many years and have been repaid with only death. Why should I falter at betraying a god who every day betrays us?

I wish I knew where it was my son lay, so that I could burn incense for his life, if any life is left. I wish I knew. Not though my breasts were pierced with spears and my hands bound with chains, not though flames burned my body would I ever put off a mother's loyalty.

O son, what place, what fate, has gotten you now? On some pathless way do you roam the fields? Has the burning ruins

	consumed your body? Do the birds of Carthage feast upon your limbs?
	For he has died, commander, in the earthquake. The death brought upon Carthage because our people disrespect your gods has fallen on my son.
T. Vulso:	Have done with lies! It is not easy to deceive Tercius Vulso. I have outmatched the wiles of mothers before. Away with vain designs; where is your son?
Apollonia:	Where is my son? Where are my brothers and sisters? Where is our god, who remains ever silent? You seek one; I seek all.
T. Vulso:	I can see it in your eyes. You stall. I do not wish to be cruel, but I will not be made a fool of. When torture comes upon you, it will drive out lies and boastful woes.
Apollonia:	If you wish to, Vulso, force me to the truth through torture, then threaten me with slavery, such as I have already been. For it is torture enough, and my prayer is to die.
T. Vulso:	Scourging, fire, and every form of torture shall force you against your will, through pain, to speak out what you are hiding, and

	from your heart I will wrench its inmost secrets; necessity is often a greater force than love.
Apollonia:	It has been done before. The past weeks were filled with whippings and brutality brought on by your poor excuses for men and soldiers. Yet we have not recanted. Bring on your flames, wounds, devilish arts of cruel pain, starvation and raging thirst, plagues of all sorts from every source, and the sword thrust deep within my innards, the dungeon's pestilential gloom. It does not matter. It has all been done before. My love admits no fear.
T. Vulso:	Love. Who do you love? Do you love your god? Do you love your son, or do you love the vanity of your own convictions? What kind of loving god treats his subjects as Christ has treated his. He is either cruel beyond belief or too weak to defend.
Apollonia:	(*hesitating*) I love . . . (*she begins to weep*) Yes, I love! I love my daughter. And I would abandon god for her, since he has abandoned me.
T. Vulso:	Daughter? You said daughter. Are you not the mother of your son?

Apollonia: (*hesitating*) My son is dead. I have no son.

T. Vulso: What assurance can you give that this is true?

Apollonia: So may all your threats and curses reign true for me and the soul of my son. May we both be buried in our own filth and may the wrath of the gods fall upon our heads in the hereafter, if my son does not lie among the dead and has not received the due of those who live no more.

T. Vulso: A strong oath. And brave. That the fates have been fulfilled by the removal of this noble's son, and that the peace of Carthage is secure, this news I will joyfully tell Hilarianus.

(*inwardly*) What will you do, Vulso? Hilarianus will believe whatever word you say, but whose word will you believe? She has confirmed her word with an oath; if the oath be false, then what is the worst that can happen to her? And yet, I have heard tell that the Christians do not make such oaths and live by the power of their "Yes" and of their "No". But then this woman did say "daughter" when she has a son, and her face, even in the midst of all her pleadings, remains calm, at peace, as if the outcome has already concluded in her favor. As if she had nothing to lose.

Now, my heart, summon up your craft, and find the truth. For look, over there stands another woman, who has not ceased to look the other way while the others stare intently at these proceedings. It is *that* woman who grieves, weeps, and groans silently; now here, now there she wanders restlessly, straining ears to catch an uttered word; that woman's fear is greater than the so-called mother here before me. Now have I need of some skill I have prepared before hand.

(*To* APOLLONIA) Other parents are more fitting to console in sorrow, but you are to be congratulated that you have lost your son, for a cruel death awaited him, cast headlong into the pit of fire beneath the statue of Cronos. You should celebrate, not mourn, for now your son is at peace, spared the humiliation. And to celebrate with you, I brought someone whom you should know well.

	Petrus Romanus, come and see your daughter.
Apollonia:	No! God, no!
	(*Enter* PETRUS ROMANUS *who proceeds immediately to run past* APOLLONIA *and fall before* PERPETUA)
T. Vulso:	Aha! Does your god lie as well as kill? (TERCIUS VULSO *pushes* APOLLONIA *aside and stands before* PERPETUA)
	Where is your son?
	(*to his attendants*) She refuses to answer. Go quickly! The sacrifice is hidden away by its mother's guile. Wherever he is hiding, in any of these rooms, hunt him out and bring him here.
	(*To* PERPETUA) Why do you look frantically about and tremble? Surely he is already dead!
Perpetua:	(*weakly*) Yes. He is surely already dead.
P. Romanus:	What are you saying? Did he not offer you the right to spare your own son? Burn

	incense to Caesar, as I tell you, fool! Recant your idiotic faith, and spare us all!
T. Vulso:	You would think the boy's grandfather would have heard the news by now that he has died in the earthquake. Now, since the boy has escaped the death he owed, we would leave you to die in peace, but some suspicion bids me stay. Your face betrays his hiding place the closer my attendants come to where he is. You have made him wallow in the filth of heretics. (TERCIUS VULSO *goes offstage where there is a commotion, and the sound of a boy's cry*)
Perpetua:	(*inwardly*) What shall I do? My mind is filled with a double fear: here, for my son; there, for my conscience and for the truth. For if I recant, my husband died in vain; my whole life has been in vain; my son, who loves his god, will live with the knowledge that it is for nothing. Better he be reunited with his father than enslaved. And yet, it tears my insides. What shall prevail? I call upon the merciless gods to witness the torment they have placed upon a mother's heart, and I call upon that true deity to give me strength. But can you, his

mother, see him given up to murderers? Can you see him sacrificed to idols?

But they have been known to lie, to trick us into recantation, all the while planning still to execute the sentence. The fire is lit, the statue prepared for the sacrifice. If not Marcus, then who?

O Perpetua, why do you waver?

(*Enter* TERCIUS VULSO *with his attendants and* MARCUS)

Apollonia: Such sacrilege! Such merciless cruelty! Is there no torture or punishment the Romans have left untried? You have profaned even your gods by how you treat your people. I will resist! I will oppose my unarmed hands against you, armed; passion will give me strength, for you deserve the blows of my fists, now let him go! (APOLLONIA *runs to* MARCUS, *attempting to free him from the soldiers, and when she is stopped by* TERCIUS VULSO *turns on him and begins to hit him*)

T. Vulso: (*to his men*) Do you hold back for a woman's futile rage? Be quick and shut her up! (TERCIUS VULSO *throws* APOLLONIA

	to the ground and his officers quickly hold her back as she attempts to again attack the commander)
Apollonia:	*(struggling with the men)* O God, heave up the earth! Rend the heavens and come down, that you may destroy these men. I despise you! I curse you, vile pagans! You ignorant sinners! You filth! On judgment day you will burn for this!
Perpetua:	Stop it! Do not curse them, for God's sake! They do not know what they are doing, and if you curse them, if you hate them, then you are just like them. We will have died in vain! We will have had faith in vain!
Apollonia:	*(weeping)* And you! Do you not see that I fight for your son when you would not? How can you call yourself a mother? How can you call this Christ a god? See? See? What faith? I cannot do this any longer! I have no more strength left. *(She casts herself at the feet of* TERCIUS VULSO*)* At your feet I fall, a slave. If violence does not convince you, then hear my cry for help! If the mother will not beg for mercy, then I will. But pity her, listen to

her prayers. The higher the gods have exalted you, the more gently bear down upon the fallen. All you need do is report to the procurator that the child is dead. He will believe you. Remember that I was his wife once, and I knew he spoke highly of you. So may all your enemies speak of you and your pure wife see you again and prolong her years with you; so may Apollo lead you on in all your battles; so may your son succeed you in success and surpass your expectations. Pity a mother! Only this one comfort is left in our affliction.

T. Vulso: You were his wife once? I remember, now. What is your name?

Apollonia: Apollonia.

T. Vulso: Then still your mouth, Apollonia. For you, there will be more to weep for before this day is through, and you have not the strength to bear it.

Perpetua, now is the time. Call for your son, and pray.

(MARCUS *runs to* PERPETUA *and they embrace*)

There he is, the terror of Carthage: a little Christian. Your father died like a commoner and yet like the noble that he was, never recanting, never begging for his life. So shall you, if I have any good judgment left.

Perpetua: (*To* TERCIUS VULSO) The way of gods and men is violence. But our way is not the same. We battle hatred with love, cruelty with kindness, evil with good. Our very god allowed himself to die in our place when we were still his enemies.

So I will not curse you, but neither will I beg you. What you have decided, you have decided. It is because you are blind. If you knew the truth, you would be more than willing to join us in the arena, to give up all you had for the sake of this god, who has come to us. So I will bless you in your blindness, for it is not you who delivers my son over to the god, but the Devil, who demands his blood and will not let us live in peace. But you will be forgiven, if you choose to see the truth.

T. Vulso: But when will I see the truth?

Perpetua: The city of Troy saw their enemies destroy them, and their queen saw the tears of a boy-king when little Astyanax was hidden in his father's tomb to no avail, only to be taken by Ulysses and thrown from the tower.

History repeats itself. The city of God is under siege, and we are Trojans now. I am telling you the Trojans died and were enslaved, yet even then, a great city arose from their bloodline. One day, just as Troy rose up into that great city, our god will raise us up to rule, and your king, along with all who now abuse us, will be cast down. Pray to our god that when we reign and judgment is finally ours, we will rule more kindly than you have ruled us.

T. Vulso: (*inwardly*) The grief and strength of this woman moves me, though I do not understand her delusions.

Apollonia: These bodies, these bodies of a people brought to dust, shall they wake to life? Shall the hands, which have demanded our blood, raise us up again? We have no hope, if we have such a god as this.

T. Vulso:	(*To* APOLLONIA) Hear your sister. Though younger, she is full of dignity far outstripping yours. At least she is faithful to her convictions. And do not blame your god, but the oracle who, by his visions, convinced Hilarianus to destroy the boy.
Apollonia:	I know him well, the devil. Contriver of fraud, a cunning sorceror whose warlike prowess never felled a single soul, but whose deceptions have looted even the greatest warriors. This is the deed of his own heart, not the gods, for Perpetua's husband was known to have performed a great miracle of healing for the Lady Faustina, when this trickster failed to do the same, and he a priest of Eshmun! He was not satisfied by the death of his competitor; now he wants his son.
T. Vulso:	Enough now. We waste too much time. It is already decided. And you should save your rantings, for the prophet also has condemned your daughter. See? You will be like your Christian sister, childless though much less faithful.

(*At this* APOLLONIA *collapses to the ground and weeps*)

	Perpetua, give me your child.
Perpetua:	Generously grant me a brief delay while I, his mother, do the last service to my son, and with a farewell embrace satisfy my grief.
T. Vulso:	Would that I might have compassion on you; but what alone I may, I will give you time. Weep your fill; weeping lightens woes.
Perpetua:	(*To* MARCUS) O sweet pledge of love, last loss of my soul for whom I used to pray: God has denied my prayers. And yet, perhaps he has not denied them. For I used to pray that he would make you like your father, and in this death you shall be. And I used to pray that you would be spared suffering, and perhaps now this will be true. You are going to your father and to a good king, and you will be spared many woes.
Marcus:	All will be well, mother. All manner of things shall be well. God is by my side. See? I have been spared.
Perpetua:	O Marcus, but I have *not* been spared!

T. Vulso: Break off your tears; great grief sets no limit to itself.

Perpetua: For my tears, Vulso, the respite I ask is small; grant me a few tears yet, that with my own hand I may close his eyes while he still lives.

(*To* MARCUS) You die a child indeed, but a man in courage and in faith. Your kingdom awaits you; go, depart in freedom.

Marcus: Remember not to pity me, mother.

(*At this* PETRUS ROMANUS *runs at* PERPETUA *and begins to beat her*)

P. Romanus: How could you? You vile wench! You fool! You are nothing but a whore like your god, the son of a whore! Disgrace! You are not my daughter! And you should die with the other fools who die like the animals they are! (TERTIUS VULSO *now pulls him off of her*) You are mad! Mad!

Perpetua: Father, why do you hit me? It is the council, the procurator, Caesar himself who should receive your blows and curses. But of course, you would lose your position. What have I done to you but damage your pride?

	And what grieves me most is that I will see my son again, yet I do not know if I shall see you. But I still love you, though you disown me. Just as I will always be a Christian and can be nothing else, so I will always be your little girl.
T. Vulso:	(*to his attendants*) There is no limit to the amount of weeping and yelling in this cursed place. Away with this whole horrid day!
	(*Exit* TERCIUS VULSO *and his attendants, the former leading away little* MARCUS. PETRUS ROMANUS *exits in their wake*)
Felicitas:	And so the storm passes, leaving in its wake only tremors. And poor Apollonia, still weeping with her daughter, to be hers no longer. And my Perpetua, condemned to be a slave like me, and slaves like me condemned to die.
	(*To* PERPETUA) All my life, I have been a slave, yet I have never seen a greater love from any master than from you since your father bought me. You made me a sister in your household. Now I only wish that I could ease your pain, for to die is better for

me. Never have I seen such rage against a people, such wickedness unleashed against the freedom of conscience. Better to die with the dying god, than live with treacherous men such as these.

May you be carried off to a good master, who will treat you with all kindness and respect. May your beauty inspire compassion, and not vile passions.

O Perpetua, what fate, what lord awaits you? To what land will he lead you? In whose kingdom shall you die?

ACT IV

Scene: Hours have passed and some prisoners sleep while others pray or converse quietly in a corner. FAUSTINA stands in the shadows, unnoticed by the others as they begin to pray.

Saturus: O Lord, how long shall it be? Come back to us! Take pity on your servants.

Felicitas: Satisfy us with your unfailing love, that we may sing for joy, even to the very end of our lives. Give us gladness in proportion to our former misery, for as many years as we have seen evil. Let us see your miracles again, and let our children see the work of your hands.

Saturus: Whosoever dwells in the shelter of the most high god

Revocatus: shall rest in the shadow of his wings. I will say to the Lord, you are my hope and my refuge: my god, in whom I trust.

Saturus: I will call to the Lord, who is worthy to be praised; so shall I be saved from my enemies.

Perpetua: (*crying out with passion*) The waves of death have closed about me. The chords of hell have encompassed me about, and the snares of death have overtaken me. In my tribulation I called to the Lord and cried to my god! And from his temple, he heard my voice cry out!

(*now pensively, as if remembering*) He reached down from above; he drew me out of deep waters. He delivered me from my enemies, from those who hated me, for they were too strong for me. They confronted me at the moment of my doom, but the Lord was my defense. He brought me to a peaceful place.

He rescued me, because he loves me.

Saturus: May the words of my mouth and the meditations of my heart be acceptable in your sight, O Lord, my strength and my redeemer.

(*All now give a collective "Amen"*)

Faustina:	(*aside*) Should I now disturb them as they pray? Look how they long for him, the god for whom they die. Yet even in their ruin, I am driven to ruin them even more. For it has fallen on me to tell the tale that Cecilia will be married--as a slave, yes, but married nonetheless--to a priest, so she might wear the dress of pagan fashion. By my craft she will be snared, married only to the beasts. So let her be deceived. It will give her but a few more moments of peace, and maybe even joy, to know her life is spared. I deem this the easier lot: death is desirable when it lacks the fear of death. But why do you hesitate to execute your orders? On him who gave them does the blame lie for this abhorrent crime. (*To the prisoners*) Where is Cecilia? (CECILIA *comes and stands before her*) Cecilia, your father has remembered you. Your fate is sealed, but be glad. In such a way does heaven regard the afflicted when you pray; it makes you ready to become a bride. Such a match can only be divine, so put off your mournful garb and don this festive array, forgetting that you are prisoner, for you are prisoner no more, but

are chosen to be married to a priest in the temple of Tanit, a good man and a high citizen of Carthage. This consummation will surely exalt you to a more exalted status.

Apollonia: Too late! Too late for treachery! Away from her! I know my husband's malice, how he was poisoned by that prophet Abdeshmun. I know she is condemned to die, and how the Romans never cease to entertain themselves by dressing up their sacrificial victims like the gods, unwilling actors on a stage suffused with blood. A morbid theater, indeed! Let her wear the pagan robes if she so chooses, but do not try and comfort her with lies.

Faustina: Although your rage will not be turned aside, still I could maintain my cause, having no desire to do what I was sent for. At first I cared not for the Christians. I cared for them as much as I would a common criminal; having seen them crucified a thousand times, they have become like chaff, inconsequential in the wind. But then a man from among you came to me, in the name of his god, without request for money or for special favors, and placed his hand upon my belly; and, in a moment, uttering no incantation but a short request, the tumor disappeared, my fever lifted, and my sight became restored. Then the plight of such pious men began to plague me, and now it culminates to an even greater pain: to repay your god by having hand in his followers' destruction. I scarce can keep from weeping.

Apollonia: (*sarcastically*) How great must be the woes you have endured for which you weep! But why weep? Tell us what tricks, what crimes my husband is devising. Must she be married to a bull, or violated in her goddess bridal dress before her throat is slit? Must she be hurled into the theater from above, or this divine marriage consummated in the pool of her own blood? For all your perversities have been displayed like this before and more, for it seems there is no end to Roman bloodlust. Speak! Speak whatever it is you hide beneath deceptive charms. Tell us! Explain what suffering you have in hand, and subtract this one from our calamities: ignorance of our fate. You see us ready to suffer death.

Faustina: I have always paid my homage to the gods, have lived for them religiously; now they repay me by forcing me to carry out their vengeance. Would that the prophet of the gods bade me instead to wander into death, to take her place and feel the fangs of animals upon my throat. For this is your daughter's fate; there is no other. Dressed as a goddess she will fight the wild beasts until she falls.

(*At this* APOLLONIA *faints, collapsing to the floor*)

Perpetua: (*inwardly*) See how the brave girl shrinks from the dress and from the woman's hand. She will not go quietly, will not go dressed as a god to be destroyed by a god and all its beasts. But look how her wretched mother, hearing again the woeful news, has fallen in a daze; her tottering frame has given way, her mind a blank. On how slender a thread her faith and body hang! And yet, she breaths; she still lives. It is a wretched thing that death has not removed her from her sorrows.

(*To* FAUSTINA) If you have any mercy in your heart, leave us for a moment. Your pagan countenance distracts us all. Let us have our goodbyes alone.

(*At this* FAUSTINA *retreats offstage*)

The very dust of Carthage thirsts for our blood. But there is hope, and it has come from that pagan woman's mouth, and may our god still bless her for it. You see the woman who has fallen prostrate there has always been an object of my prayers, my companion, a comfort in affliction, my resting place; and Cecilia is her entire offspring, the only voice that calls her mother.

O obstinate men! Rebellious against the god! They would separate the two and from it make two deaths: one, a living death. Her mother, unhappy soul, has lost her faith. She is not ready in such weakness to lose all, but I have deemed it fit that I should take her daughter's place. The girl is just my age and just my height.

Husband, I am coming to you.

(*To* CECILIA) Remain alive, my sister, and strengthen your mother.

Cecilia: I am slow of speech, but I will say this: I should die, Perpetua, not you. I am ready to stand and die for the truth, willing to submit to whatever beast they send for me.

Perpetua: Stay your courage. The Lord is not a god who needs your blood. He sees your heart, that you are willing; this is enough. He has given you the way out. Live, for your mother's sake. I have nothing left to keep me here, no reason I should stay and you should go.

I saw it in a vision, that I am meant to die, but when I heard I was to be a slave, I thought that I had been mistaken: God had not spoken to me. Yet now I see how the dream must be fulfilled: to take your place, to let you live, and follow in his steps.

Cecilia: Is any part of my suffering still unknown to me? To whom were you given as a slave? Whom shall I call master?

Perpetua: To Tercius Vulso you will go, a servant to the general.

Cecilia: Is that why you so willingly replace me? Shall I go and be the slave of him who took away your son? Will the hands that threw his body to the flames touch mine as well? I would rather die!

Perpetua:	No! Do not say it, for God will spare your purity. I know his wife. She will throw him to the beasts before he touches you, for her jealousy is as great as her many kindnesses. And she believes as we do, though in secret. She will care for you. So rejoice and be glad! You will be well.
	(*Enter* FAUSTINA)
Faustina:	(*To* CECILIA) And even more good news: Your mother goes to serve my father, who is blind and the years she has lived will help her understand him. Believe me, this is not another lie I have devised, but the truth. I have heard my husband swear it with an oath, when he bid me come and bring you to your doom. Vibia Perpetua, I will make sure that you often go to visit Apollonia, your friend.
Cecilia:	You call me Perpetua. Then you overheard?
Faustina:	Yes, I overheard. My heart became like wax, melting within me as I heard it: no love to match it have I ever witnessed. It is I who should serve you. I should be thrown to the beasts, and you should rise again.

	I swear to you, if you both so choose, then I will keep this to myself on pain of death, on the words of the vilest oath, and by all the gods. No one will ever know.
	(To CECLIA) You forever will remain Vibia Perpetua.
	(To PERPETUA) And you are Cecilia, but only for a little while.
Perpetua:	How can I offer you my gratitude? Fear not because we die. For the god who healed you will forgive, and I shall not forget this kindness.
	(To all prisoners) Even now the footsteps of those who usher in our deaths have reached my ears. Many of our brothers have died in prison waiting for this day. Sickness has robbed them of the chance to manifest their love, even though they have been spared many torments. Yet even more blessed are we, to die for the one who died for us.
	Everyone, be ready! They are here.
	(Enter PUDENS *with various soldiers)*

Pudens: Lady Faustina, the magistrate asks why you delay. I have come to bring the prisoners to their deaths, though I am blessed to see them one last time. Saturus, Revocatus, Felicitas, Cecilia; the arena waits.

(PUDENS *stops the soldiers from binding Perpetua*)

Perpetua: To Christ I am summoned. I go willingly. No need for chains. Lead on, O Christ. I hold not back. I follow my master. But the fates, which you profess, will follow me into this city when I am gone. They are sent from the mouth of the creator god, whom we worship. And I speak it not as a curse, but as a warning: upon the seas no peace shall come. They will rage with the winds and engulf your ships; and you, even when safe at home again, will fall to war and fire and tremor. And when they come remember me, that I came from God, and turn to him.

Do you hear? The masses crying out for blood. Pudens, why do you hesitate? Why are you afraid? Be at peace. They wait, so we must go and quench their thirst for violence.

	Felicitas, my faithful servant, look! God has seen it that we die together, sisters.
Felicitas:	I am bound, but never have I felt so free, for I am with you. Sweet to the one who mourns are others who also mourn. Lighter is the sting of tears when accompanied by a throng of weeping. At least together we shall increase our strength and bear the lot all must eventually endure.
Revocatus:	Many do not choose to face this lot. It comes upon them unawares, and all their revelry and worldly lusts are worthless in that moment. It strips them bare. Remove those blessed with heaps of gold; remove him who ploughs rich fields with a hundred oxen; and the downcast spirits of the poor rise again. Rich or poor, we are all naked when dead. We only go the way that they who condemn us now will go someday, though they bid us go ahead. And for that very act, Rome itself will one day pay us homage.
Perpetua:	(*kneeling beside* APOLLONIA) My friend, I know you cannot hear me, but rest assured that I will be forever honored dying with these Christian women, who have rivaled Deborah in their strength, Dido in their

wisdom. Yet my one regret is that I will not behold your face when you awake to see your daughter there, as if resurrected from the grave. And when you do, remember that I loved you, that you were like a mother to me. And though your faith has wavered, and you do not understand, perhaps you will, soon enough.

(CECILIA *and* FAUSTINA *begin to cry*)

Do not weep for me! Let Faustina, who sheds tears for a lost daughter of Rome, weep not for me but for herself and for her people.

(*To* CECILIA) And you, weep for your enemies, who do not know the judgment they are heaping up upon themselves.

Goodbye, Perpetua.

(PERPETUA *and* CECILIA *embrace as* FELICITAS, REVOCATUS, *and* SATURUS *are lead away by the soldiers*)

Pudens: You who are called Cecilia, come. It is time.

(*Exit* PERPETUA, PUDENS, *and* FAUSTINA)

Cecilia: It is by the light of burning martyrs that Christ is glorified and seen by men. O wretched world, perverted justice! The innocent die to appease the wicked. But one day, son to mother and mother to son will point to the place where our ruins lie prostrate saying, "This is the city that destroyed the saints, this the empire that kills the prophets and never fails to call the righteous man a heretic, where the smoke of burning corpses curled high to heaven, where the foul vapors hung." And Carthage will be no more. Rome will be no more. But the word of our god will still remain, and his people will still stand when all else falls.

(*kneeling beside* APOLLONIA, *attempting to revive her*) Mother, please. Wake! For they will soon come for us to take us to our new homes. Wake up, mother! Please, wake! There is no need to faint. I live!

Mother . . .

ACT V

Scene: In the prison, APOLLONIA *and* CECILIA *are alone, still waiting to be escorted to their new lives as slaves.*

Enter PUDENS

Pudens: O cruel fate, harsh pitiable horror! What crime so savage, so grievous in all of war has Apollo ever seen as this? What first should I tell amidst my lamentations, of which saint's courage should I boast?

Apollonia: Whosoever woes you weep, you will weep mine. Each feels the weight of his own disaster only, but I the disasters of them all; for me do all things perish.

Pudens: Perpetua is slain; her son thrown into the fiery pit; her teacher eaten by a leopard; and her slave destroyed by bulls. But each met doom with a noble spirit.

Cecilia: Expound their deaths in order and relate this twofold crime: the sacrifice of innocence and the death of saints. Out with it! Tell us the tale.

Pudens: There was, in our city ages ago, a great bronze statue of Cronus extending its arms, so that each infant sacrifice, when cradled there, was rolled down and fell into a gaping pit of fire. Such tophets came into disuse when the Romans overtook us, and they who regularly sacrifice their own victims for sport, found other sacrifices too distasteful. They readily approve of children thrown to feed the lions, but a formal feeding of a god is no longer such as the divinities require. Yet for this festival, the priests erected such an idol in memory of the glorious days of Carthage, and at its feet again, a pit of fire.

Now the stands were thronged with people, and with stately step the crafty priest approached his god, and in his wake a slave carried little Marcus, who was bound, and with no frantic wailing or thrashing of his limbs was he brought to meet his fate and placed upon the idol's arms. And lying on the god, he turned his keen gaze now here, now there, undaunted in spirit, his face at peace. He moved the crowd to silence, when Abdeshmun took

	his place beside the boy. As the priest rehearsed the words and prayers appointed him and summoned the cruel gods to the sacrifice, of his own will did Marcus wrench himself from the prophet's grip and roll into the pit without a cry.
Cecilia:	What Cretan, what barbarian has ever caused a crime like this, or what uncivilized tribe has ever dared it? Perhaps the sacrifice of children satiates the gods of other lands, but I have not known it until now. No wonder Abram did not seem surprised when summoned by an unknown god to sacrifice his only son, for it seems the gods would have it so; and yet, this god did stay the father's hand, declaring it a sin if it be done. The test complete, the god was stilled by faith in heart and not by knife in hand.

Now, who will take up the little martyr? Who will take his limbs and consign him to a tomb? |
| *Pudens*: | What limbs are left within the pit? His bones were burnt to ash and mixed with stone and coal and dust. |

Cecilia: And yet God knows the ashes that are his. So tell us now, how did the others meet their ends?

Pudens: Lamentably but bravely. The day of their victory over death shone forth, and they proceeded to the amphitheater as if to an assembly, joyous and of brilliant countenance. But when brought to the gate, they were forced to put on clothing: the men that of the priests of Saturn and the women that of goddesses, but they resisted. Perpetua spoke first and said, "We have come this far of our own choosing, for the very reason that our liberty might not be taken from us. Will you force us now, at the very end, to do what is against our conscience? We have yielded our bodies to be punished by you, that we might not do any such thing: we have agreed on this with you." And the logic of her argument won over, allowing them to enter in the ring and die just as they chose.

Saturus perished first, and in so perishing, ascended the ladder into his god's eternal kingdom, where he was waiting for Perpetua. The minute he stepped in the arena, a leopard lunged at him. The saintly deacon saw the beast approach and was given only a moment to lift his hands in praise to heaven, before being knocked down, his throat ripped out. Revocatus, on seeing his beloved teacher, ran to his side and in desperation even tried to wrestle with the beast, receiving for his efforts the jaws of that same leopard. Mortally wounded, he fell beside the body of his friend.

The women were given over to a mad bull, released upon them as they were led forth. It tossed Perpetua first, poor lady, to the ground upon her face. And when she arose, she saw her Felicitas crushed and gored, wallowing in her blood. So she ran to her servant, gave her her hand, and lifted her up so that they might both stand together against the beast. When they were struck again, Felicitas gave up her spirit, and Perpetua, being wounded but not yet killed, crawled to her sister's side once more and kissed the cold and bloodied cheek, that they might consummate their martyrdom with a kiss of peace. Then, to the astonishment of the people, she stood and raised her hands to heaven and held the masses awe-struck.

A young gladiator, barely a man, was dispatched to finish her off with his sword. And when she saw him, Perpetua lowered her hands and approached with confidence, her face radiant in the dying splendor of her beauty. Some, her beauty moved; some, her tender youth; some, the shifting changes of her fortune; but one and all were filled with terror, wonder, and pity at her dauntless courage.

And then he reaches her. The maid does not shrink back but, facing the stroke, stands there with a stern courageous look. A spirit so bold strikes the hearts of all and--strange prodigy--the boy is slow to kill. He hesitates, as if struck by some unspoken word. He stares. His right hand trembles with the sword, yet he must kill. For if he fails, then might he, too, be struck and killed by his superiors. But he cannot kill her, cannot mar her beauty. So, gently and with her eyes on his, she grasps his wavering hand and guides it to her throat.

The blood, like the sigh that then escaped the crowd, burst forth. The martyr fell. Some within the crowd began to weep. But many mourned her with a timid lamentation, for fear that they might be accused of sympathy for Christians. Others cheered their victory. And the shed blood seeped between the cracks; instantly, the savage mound sucked it down and drank the whole draught of gore.

Cecilia: O brave and blessed martyrs! In death, as in life, they were like their Lord. I am blessed to bear the name Perpetua among my pagan masters. Yet among our people, I shall remain Cecilia, for I will not rob her of the glory of her death.

Pudens: We must never tell the extent of her sacrifice, lest you be in danger. But I know that while imprisoned she wrote down many of her thoughts and dreams, and I will make them known and add to them the manner of her death, so that at least, though not proclaiming that you live because of her, the world will see her in her glory. Already they speak of that nameless woman in the ring, who raised her hands to heaven to receive the gladiator's sword.

Apollonia: Carthage, city of my discontent. Go now and be at peace. You have assuaged the thirst of the gods, the jealousy of Caesar. Let your prosperity now see no end. A maiden and a boy have fallen; the war against them won.

I shall not mourn their loss alone, though once I longed to die, for fear of losing all and being left alone. Whereas death, the object of my prayers, came with speed and savage violence everywhere; me it shunned. Though I sought it in the midsts of swords and pyres, the prisons and the wild beasts, it still evaded my eager search. No foe, no raging god, no fire has consumed my limbs. Yet, now, I am overwhelmed with gratitude that it has never found me, for the saint has won me my daughter.

I have been a fool and worthy of death, for I threw myself at the feet of my enemies and cursed them to their faces. I cursed the name of our god. I did not understand the dying god and how it is in sacrifice and death that love is most faithfully portrayed.

Pudens: Hasten now, for already your masters wait with expectation. After many weeks you have found a kind of freedom in the very leaving of these prison walls.

Exeunt omnes.

ABOUT THE AUTHOR

Seraphim George's work bridges nature, faith, and the human experience. He has published poetry in multiple literary journals and wrote an award-winning novel. Seraphim continues to write poetry and novels while working in Communications for non-profits. He spends his free time in church, on the water, and in the written word, not to mention raising his three children with his wife, Juliana, and his cat, Kimchi. Christian Women is his first written play.

To read more of his work and find out more about him, you can visit his website: www.seraphimgeorge.com.

www.ingramcontent.com/pod-product-compliance
Lightning Source LLC
Chambersburg PA
CBHW071315040426
42444CB00009B/2018